I0531867

I'm Writing To Tell You

I'm Writing To Tell You

POETRY BY JAHA ZAINABU

MAMA'S
KITCHEN
PRESS

I'm Writing To Tell You
© 2022 Robin Reed
ISBN: 979-8-9853373-5-8

Published by Mama's Kitchen Press
Austin, TX / Los Angeles, CA
mamaskitchenpress.com

First Trade Paperback Original Edition, 2022

All rights reserved. No part of this publication may be
reproduced, distributed, or transmitted in any form or by
any means, including photocopying, recording, or other
electronic or mechanical methods, without the prior written
permission of the publisher, except in the case of brief
quotations embodied in critical reviews and certain other
noncommercial uses permitted by copyright law.

Manufactured in the United States of America

Cover Art by Jaha Zainabu
Cover Concept by Annie Cercone
Cover and Layout Design by Emily Anne Evans

To my ancestors

Table of Contents

I'm Writing To Tell You

Word

The first draft of a poem
Should be scribbled in a mind
That knows its body ain't free
All that truth should feel like gallstones
Like a bag of rocks on fire in your belly
And gotta come out
Don't
Then you die
Don't
Then the whole world ain't safe

Ain't that a poet's job
Sweep this world up
Clean as it can get

A poem should be ugly
Should start off wrinkled, loud, innocent and bloody
Should taste like Flint water
Should be dense as Georgia dirt
Opaque as L. A. sky
A poem should leave traces

All over your carpet
All up on your couch

All these babies dying
Some killing they own selves
Women missing everyday
Police ain't never been no good

Even a happy poem got pulp
Even a love poem got seeds

A poem should have lines carved out
Should ask a question it can't answer
It should solve an old problem
Should dare you to dream a world
Outside your little ole lives
Should make you remember that hell is here
Heaven too
Heaven right here too
A poem should tell you
Ain't no life easy

My grandmother, five times great
Was a slave on this good land

Probably picked cotton
Probably forced to have some white man's child
Maybe died tied to a tree
Never knowing her own name
A poem should take you back
Make you wonder
If your nightmare
Ain't really a memory

A poem should sit with you
On the bus stop
On a rainy night and wonder
If Jesus see all this
Should ask what's taking him so long
Oh you ain't ready
Ain't ready to wonder if God and the devil
Had theyselves one good ole laugh
I tell you

A poem should offer you its hand to squeeze
While you release boils and flesh and clots
One story at a time

Me

I am a river
That flows into bigger rivers
The rabbit that runs across graves
The subtle shake
The simple quiver

I am a chorus
A question
An unloaded gun
A bullet nearby

I am a holy war
A quiet riot

Hustle

Will work for food
Will fuck for money
Will suck for a shower and a night out
Anal for a month's rent
I will be your pretty girl
I will call you Daddy
You can be my Superman
Keep me safe off the ground

Do you know concrete women like me
Do you know how we live
Do you know what we do
For a tampon
A cheeseburger
A shake

I will kiss you slow
I will wear my hair long
You want a skinny woman
You wanna see how fast I skinny

I'm Writing To Tell You

You seen me before
Women like me
Sleeping on bus stops
Under trees
No shoes

I clean up well
I pretty up nice
I sex real good
I have given up on this life can't you tell

Tell me what you want me to be
And I'll be
Tell me what to say
Take me to your place
I'll sit nice and quiet

Do you want a queen
Do you want a whore
Do you want a slut or a cunt
Do you want me spread all over your body
Do you want to know how I got here
Do you want to know my story

Will you give me a hug
Some fries
May I keep the change
Will you save my life

Come through

Somebody bring me a river
Bring me an ocean
A lake
Some water I can walk into and clean myself
And only come out if I want to

Somebody tell me what you know
About carrying this kind of weight
Not these hips
These thighs
I'm talking about this skin
This Black
This woman
Tell me how you feel
When you see this body done wrong

Somebody bring me a hole to crawl into
One that's made just for me
Where I can use it
When holding my stress and yours too
Get to be too much for me

Where somebody at
Somebody to grease this scalp
And lotion these legs

Come through, somebody
Come through

Somebody bring me a pen
I can write down
All I want to say
So don't nobody forget

Come through, somebody
Somebody tall or short
Fat or skinny
With freckles or without
Somebody with some get up and get ready
Somebody with some act right about theyself

Come through, somebody

You see these scars
I been here before
Was a wolf and a bear
A bee and a tree
I put in all types of work

I just wanna rest now
Come through, somebody
Come hold my hand
While I fall asleep

Necessary

I am a necessary
A remember
A lily
A forgive

I am a healing
A bold
A remix
A shy
A plenty

You see these fingers
You know the spells that they cast
You know my motherfucking name
The syllables in each whisper
Way the power rolls off your tongue
You know

I am a strong
A work overtime
I am a thick

You know how I woman
You can tell

I am a bend
A reach
A stretch so far to the clouds
I am a nap
A sleep so good like heaven
Like rent paid
Like water too

A wet
A love so dripping
You have to be grown enough for all this heat

I am a morning
A sun
I am the earth reconnecting itself
To God

Us

Daydreams are dangerous in my crawling fingers
Daddylonglegging up my sides
Time is like red on my palms
Melting marrow in my bones
And there is me
And too many hours unattended
Left to my imagining
Laughter so easy
This us makes sense

Who else would we hold this free
Until grits and eggs
Daybreak biscuits
Buttery go bad
We blanket the morning sun
Enough is still to come
Thigh on thigh
Mouth on neck
Like it always begin this way
You hum melody
I serenade

Stevie Wonder
Luther love
Midday
Morning
Before supper
After
There is always a ready
Itchy for the again
We are the softest place we know
We separate
Then gallup to reconnect
I am too classy to teach my doggie on open mic
Too together to put my pearls before the sign up sheet
Ever peppered
Lawrys
Louisiana
Rooster
Fire love come simple to seasoned women
Relax in my Mona Lisa
Until I unveil the Basquiat
Watch this grown woman
Murder your shero

We Pac Man
Super Mario
Lovers go back so far
Confidence come comfortable
We unlimited data
Waiting to be stored
Appetizers
Entrees
We are exhausting in my mind

Push

We learned to push love away through imitation
We saw early our fathers and brothers
Second us to their cars and gods
Our tenacious rhythm of articulating
Our womanist sensibilities
Through Double Dutch chants and house play
With candy cigarettes

But why did we have to choose a struggle
Be Black or be woman
Like color and pussy don't connect
Be gay or be Christian
Like love and religion ain't the same
Fuck nasty or be wife
Like legs wrapped so squeezed around my man's waist
Say I ain't his queen
Hair nappy or bone straight
Like how steady my comb stick
Say whether I can fight a dog off my back

What do you know about where our lives intersect
Like we can't have faith and be afraid
Like we can't forgive and remember how dirty you
played
Like we can't be devil afraid of our reflections
And look into our eyes at the same time
And know how magnificent we are

Safe

He holds the loud of my love
Safe in his protest
Careful as a boy
With a bubble
And a sword

He ain't nobody's boy
He be drumming my blues away
He a man
Mama I got me a man
Ain't afraid of my blues

Monsters ride with me
Telling me to forgo tomorrows
Say death the best rest yet

He be daring them demons
To take off them masks
He be baitin' 'em y'all
Callin' 'em punk ass bitches and shit

On my darkest days
I turn off all the lights
I wrap up in a robe
Like I am something to hide

He say
Baybeeee please
You ain't got to change
A gotdamn thang

Me too

And so what of joy
What of food
What of the taco truck on LaBrea on Venice
Because cheese is important too

A man I thought I could have grown to love
Chose crack over me
I know it was not about me
I was hurt anyway
Had to steal back my Impala
From the Snooty Fox
Back of my t-shirt
Bloody from the abortion

And so what of ugly
Of my ugly
Ugly versions of myself
I have been to other people
Ways I have bullied
Have abused
Have pawned the unhealed parts of myself onto him

Too many hims to mention
The random hims
The ones that came and went
Too many went
I went too

And what do I tell my son
Of all of my going
About the night I tried to leave forever
Told myself that he would be better off
The voices all agreed

It took me nine months to apologize
I tried to explain to him
The heavy of my sadness that night
On so many nights before
He told me honest as he could
Said it was ok
Said he understood
I hope he never understands

Ain't I a whole person
Ain't my whole life important too
Is my life just the sum of my mistakes

But what of my beauty
My dedication
My loyalty
And the priceless friends I have
What of that

What of all the ways that I am othered

All the ways I like myself
In the face of all the othering
What about my big love for me
For the ways I touch
Touch you
Touch myself too
Don't I deserve my own touch
And what about pleasure
And what is the distinction
Between pleasure and joy
Ain't I worthy of joy and smile

What of the song of myself
What I see when I look into a mirror
The battlefield of emotions
Going on inside my head

Brother called me his wisdom
Told me to call him God
But what about me
And the I am who lives inside
Can a woman be a God too

Can a man run my bath
What of the ways I weigh
What you think of me
Over how I value myself
My good time
My girlish grin
My unpainted toes
Even the anxiety
Even the depression
Even the moods
Many as they be

What of all the days I cancel the brunch
Decide against the shower
And the laundry
And the dishes too
All the ways I choose
Not to contort myself
Shrink my skin and bones
To fit into your flask
Like a secret in your pocket
And what of this new day
When my no is holy
When my yes is freedom
This a whole sweet life ain't it
A whole canvas
I paint myself

A run on for Sabrina Fulton and other mothers when a t-shirt is not enough

Sabrina Fulton cannot carry her grief to the white woman at the phone company and explain that a man killed her son and got away with it.

Because who cares about Black boys anyway? And even though the story is no longer on the news, his picture is still on the coffee table next to the Bible and the Vogue mags and bills.

And is it possible to get an extension on the mortgage and car payments because sleeping on the couch for a month straight and going nowhere fast shouldn't cost as much anyway right?

But who understands this except someone who has tasted thorns for breakfast because the doctor said eat something and take something and try to get some sleep?

But who can sleep and think straight when every time eyes close, floating Arizona tea cans grow monster ears?

And who can go outside and see teenagers wearing shirts that say they remember and they will never forget?

Who can form sentences and why are mothers supposed to be this strong and pray this hard about Black boys and girls who are supposed to come home every night and not be shot down and killed?

Our Black boys. Our Black girls. And where are our girls' faces on shirts? And why are shirts so necessary? And dead babies are not fashion.

Our children are supposed to live and not die. And this was not God's plan. Not all this. What God would plan this? What God would need an angel so badly it would have to take ours? How could anyone need a writing prompt when there are babies' lives to save and streets to walk down, teachers to meet with and drug dealers to cuss out and hair to braid and womens' bodies found dead in Atlanta?

And are white boys and girls needed in heaven too?

For Leelah Alcorn

Leelah
Leelah
For the way your name
Gives my mouth permission to sing and smile
Leelah
I will call you a girl
A she
I will sew a dress in your honor

I am sorry you had no place you felt comfortable
Falling your shoulders
Humming your butterfly of a name
Fingering your path through this sand of a world

What an ending to the beginning of your life
Your life
Yours
I will listen
As tribute to you

I will care

I will cry
I will fling these useless tears to sky

I will why for you
I will how come in your stead
I will pull hair and hold heart for you
For you and the next boy or girl
Who feels trapped in this box of an earth
Judgements too rigid
Rules too tightroped to tippy toe
Leelah, sweet Leelah
Rest, Leelah
Fly

This is our America

There was another poem I planned to write today

It never fully formed
Something to do with daisies and or lilies
Had the perfect line I kept repeating
To remind myself to add as finish
I can't remember it now

Not now
Not after watching video of boys in Steubenville, Ohio
Witness a sixteen year old girl
Being raped
Urinated on
Watch her pass out
See her body lie on the floor
And laugh
Make jokes
Take video and photo

My measly love poem would be whipped cream

Spread over dirt pie

These are our boys we are rearing
They called her "dead girl"
Dead girl
"She's deader than O. J.'s wife" he said
They laughed
"You know how I know she's dead?
They peed on her and she didn't move"
They laughed
"There was a wang in her ass and she didn't move
There's usually a reaction to that"
Somehow that was funny too

This is America
This is how we have taught our boys to feel about women
About our so what bodies they want to control
Ohio
Steubenville
High School
Football
Party

She wasn't dead
Dead girl wasn't dead
Maybe she wished she was
When she heard the coach say
She made up the rape to explain
Why she came home that way
That way
Came home that way

Watch her unconscious body
Being carried across the room
One boy holding her arms
Another her feet
Dead girl
They called her dead girl

Dead girl is not a nickname
A girl earns at a party
Like Barbie or Squeak
Long legs or Freckles

That way
Came home that way

This rape culture we live in
Where jocks are as untouchable as the devil
This victim blaming curse of a country

We did this
We reared those boys to rape
To laugh and videotape the funny of it all
To post photos of a girl's body
Being carried across the room

Out of the way

Dear Jaha

Loving yourself is showing up in the world as your word
As your commitment to family, art, justice
It is knowing that love matters
Your words
Your hugs and hellos

It is not being swallowed by the headlines of the day

Even today when
White Mississippi teen runs over Black man for fun
Police say it is not a hate crime

When you cannot manage the lows
Or come down from the highs
Loving yourself is forcing your feet to stop moving
Your knees to bend
Your body to still
Allowing yourself to be
As the ugliest moments wash over your head

I do not know that the waters will not drown you
Only this is true

A lifetime of last times until the next time
And deciding in every right now
To choose love

Loving yourself is knowing
Your love is powerful enough to hold itself up
Loving yourself is using your hands to serve someone
else
What did you do today
How did you show up in the world so that someone
else is better
A better that matters and makes a difference in the
world
So that someone else is better

A better that matters and makes a difference
In the world
On your block

Did you hold a hand
Did you give a heart
Love yourself enough to reach down past your words
And give your whole heart beating
To at least some one

Did you listen to a story or blow a nose
Did you let a stranger share her God with you
O Jaha, that is the best
Watch her face rainbow after the telling of each blessing
Did you unbusy your moment long enough
To hear him say I love you
Did you see his shoulders fall
Before you turned away

Loving yourself is being committed to someone else's
win
It is knowing when enough is enough
And when time to rest
To let love fill itself up again in you

Loving yourself is giving it away
It is knowing that your whole life
Everything you know and everything you don't
All that you have forgiven
And everything you hold
Is now
And now again

To love yourself is to know
That life is only right now
And everything you carry into the next right now
Is everything you carry
Into the next right now

Preach, woman

Do not tell me about your calling from God
To heal even a corner of this world
With words
With fingers touching
Grabbing
Reaching into the leprosy of hate and fear
And then tell me that God would have you disappear
That God would dare unbreast you
What God would silence your woman story

Who can sing like bird
Better than bird
What will clean the air more thorough than tree
Mountain will not apologize
For being in the way
Ocean has yet to make amend
For the souls that it has swallowed

We adjust to the night under moon
And her womanist ways
She does not offer disclaimer

When she steps naked to the sky
For not being sun

And so why do we beg forgiveness
With all we have to give and say
We carriers of life and world

Spit shine your uterus
And set it on the pulpit

For love

I will be for love today
Living just one life
Through many incarnations
And the sanctified souls who hold my head
Will not ever allow me to forget
The lessons of my past

But when I don't remember
And am pulled into the drama
Of my bygone

The great grandmother of my angel
A crackled blackblue spirit
Gently sticks me with her crown
And I scream ouch
Don't poke me like that

I will lay my blues to rest today
Swear never pick them up again
Except to remind tomorrow
The hours that I fell

How I got this scar
And why some
Say all the right words
Graduate from all the right schools
But only get so far
From today
Not the contents of my wallet
Or weight
Not my relationship status or work
My circumstances shall not decide my worth
I am flawless

Gaining understanding new
On my journey at every turn

I began in the mind of God
Who is beginningless
So I too am without a start

The angels up in heaven
The stars in the sky know it's true
So if you don't too
Then you are in the few
Because I am alright with me

With freckles
Thick thighs
Nappy hair and big feet
And the grown woman way
My breasts hang and booty pokes a little

I am more than woman
More than stories and poems
Than Black and painter
I am more than water and daughter

I am not just chest and blood
Bones and flesh

I am that I am
As all of you are me too
And I am you

So what is it to be Christian or Catholic
Jewish or Muslim
Science of mind or Bahai

It doesn't even matter
That some do not recognize
The awesome outstanding of the Most High

My religion is love
So don't ask me what I am
It should only be important to you
That I exist at all
If all the things around you
Should quickly fade away

Who would you believe in
What would you stand for
Today

Hiding

There's a lot of hiding
There's a lot of pretending to be ok
There's a lot of debating about whether or not
The meds have ever done any good

There's a lot of needing to do something with your
fingers
There's a lot of crying
There just is

There's a lot of not being able to explain to anyone
around you
How the sadness weighs a ton
Or what the tears are for anyway
And so
There's a lot of hiding

There's a lot of wanting to reach out but then
What would you say that you haven't said before

There's a lot of knowing that this is not the right time
To break down
To sleep that final sleep

There's a lot of wanting to explode
There's very little rest
There's too much sleep

There's a lot of time
Time
Time time
Time to remember all the time
There's a lot of time to count

There's a lot of counting
There's a lot of rushing past mirrors
There are a lot of covers on the floor
There are a lot of clothes on the floor
There are books on the floor
There is very little cleaning up

There is a lot of wanting to be able to sleep
There are so many hours going by so slowly

There are so many weird awake dreams
About flying
About rats
About mice
About fires
About hands

There is a lot of being afraid to go to sleep
Because there are so many monsters
There are all these fingers
Moving fingers
There's a lot of wanting to stop writing
Poetry
Stories
Words
Musings
Blogs
Stuff
Stuff stuff
Journal entries
Letters
Email

There's a lot of wanting all the stuff off the floor

There's a lot of wanting help
There's little asking for it
There's no desire to go into the hospital again
There is a need to
There's all this this
There's all this that
There's all this
Down down down down
There is all this smile
When someone says how are you
There's all this I am ok
There's all this nowhere to look

There is all this want to change the furniture
There is no energy to do it
There is all this want to tie yourself up
There is all this staring at stuff
At pills
At plants
At photos
At pills
Pills

There is all this talking to yourself
There is all this knowing that this is the wrong time to
leave
There is all the nothing to say
There is all the wanting to say something
There is all this wanting it to go away
There is all this knowing it won't
There is all this wanting

911

This poem is not about revolution
Or Malcolm or Tupac or revenge
Or an attack on America or even her own injustice
It's not even about Assata

But about a mother who rides the blue line at 6
Gets off every morning at the Imperial station
Is a nurse who loves her son even still
Held him in a light only she and God could seem to
see

He was 16 and licorice black with a handsome smile
And perfect teeth
Just like his daddy

And was shot and killed by another man and woman's
boy
That heavy on her back somehow not being enough
Today she goes about her days remembering
On the eve of her only child's services
While his body wait alone and cold beyond a

comforters cure
His murderer captured only by karma
Maybe
Emptied his body
Spray painted his casket in red letters
Old English font now tattooed on the chest of her
memory

This poem is not about the courage it takes to
remember
He always kissed her good night
Ate greens with ketchup
Loved fish with his grits

This is not about Rodney King or Daryl Gates
Latasha Harlins or Stacey Koon
Not even about Soon Ja Du
This poem has nothing to do with Watts 1965
Not really

But kinda

In a way it is about a brave little girl out in Montebello
Who was beautiful and 4
Who sat in her room and counted
Dos, tres, quatro, cinco
Loudly under all her pillows

While her father repeatedly stabbed her mother
And then left
And she tearlessly embraced her mother's
Bleeding, dying body
Patted her hand, rocked and said

James te pueden hacer dano
Dios te va hacer bonita

No one will hurt you
God will make you pretty

There are many stories
If by chance they should all be told one day
There will be many more
Even after that
This isn't about La Revolucion Mexicana
I already told you that

Only the revolution that occurs in the souls of us
Who still love the spirits of those of whom
We cannot see

We see these heroes on the bus
On the train
At the light
Honoring the memory of those faces
That may never flash across the evening news
And those faces that do

I pray that when I have passed away
I will have created grand memories enough
To sustain my loved ones well

I pray that in the break of morning clear
They will breathe without having to be reminded
Accepting finally

That there is an inevitable death
That comes with living
Though religions and philosophies do best they can
At explanation
They will not ever have power enough to prevent

Having lived life time over and again
I have found laughter to be truest friend
For therein lies at evil's demise
God within us all

This poem
If indeed it is a poem at all
Is about
Dancing on hurt feet

Jaha Zainabu

This is my body

There are two mirrors in my home
And too many days go by in a row
When I avoid them both
I am my own worst trigger
I am my very best cheerleader

Loving myself is acknowledging
There are times
I am not loving myself

There are times I stand in the glory
Of the kindness of my heart
The well of my art
Steady of my dedication
To justice and freedom for all
The curve and soft of my frame
Reach of my fingers

And there are times I long for winter
To hide my body
Under colorful clothes

I wear layers to cover
The poke of my stomach
The dead of my fish
Spread of my thighs
Pollution in my air
Fluffy of my face
My hips
The starvation of my children
The discard of my elders

I'm Black and I'm proud
I'm Black and I'm proud
My country tis of thee
Sweet land of liberty

I shout my mantras
And cover myself
With all this fabric
Under all this smog
With all these propositions
Blinged in all these
Stripes and stars

In hopes that you will be fooled
By my fancy politics
Into loving me too

This is my body
Take
Eat

This is my body
This is my mind to make up
My vote to cast
My right to choose

Don't stand in my way
With your magic wand words
To guilt me out of my grief
My doubt

This is my body
Hung
Stolen
Burned
Sold

My body that I have worked into frenzy
Fire
Spin
Worry
Over what you think

They keep taking my children
Killing my babies
My Trayvon
My Marco
My Latasha
My Hadiya

Kimani Gray
Sixteen years old
Flatbush
Shot down by police

This is my body
I love my arms
And deport my Mexicans
Paint my toes
And cut off my homosexuals

I dye my hair
And rape my women
I work out my abs
And imprison my men

This is my body
This bread
This red

Do this in remembrance of me

Sweet home

God holds the hearts of women in a special place I feel
The benevolent eye that watches the sparrow watch us
I know
Still the conversations of victim, defeat and not enough
show up
Harmoniously, in whispers, often, today

We understand, as if understanding were cure
Through long work shifts, sore feet and bills due
Through birthdays and school plays
We are hopeful inside closets where we cry
On the lawn chairs where we laugh
About the nothing

We know we are enough
Every day the lessons to be learned
Still we are big girls longing jump rope and recess
Tetherball and gossip

We are strong
We are our mothers and grandmothers

I stand in front of my mirror
Full breasts
Hips that carried my son
A belly that rested his head
Still the not enough shows up

Sometimes I listen
But sometimes
I don't

Dear Isaac

What if the story was never your father's
What if the lesson to the world was meant from your
vantage
How old were you
At what moment did you know
The story sings his faith and courage
But what about you
Was there no wiggle
No struggle to escape
When did you give in
Who saw the ram first
Who heard the voice
What was it like the second after
Did he speak on the walk down Moriah
What did he say
Did you run tell your mother
Your beautiful mother
Who was barren for so many years
Did you trust him after that
How protected did you feel
Did your mother sing to you that night

Rub your head while you slept
Did you flinch for years after every time he called you
son

What did he tell you about his god to make you stay
Please tell me, Isaac
What words did he say
Tell me about that kind of faith

O it is a lovely song
How he had a son
Was ready to sacrifice his only one
But you were not
They could not have forgotten about Ishmael
What about your brother
It is like that, you know
With women and children
We are forgotten and dispensable

You ever wonder why you
Why your life was up for gamble

What if he had not heard the voice or saw the ram
What if he acted too soon
Then what
Then what about you
Don't mind me brother
I was always inquisitive

What if the miracle was due to your faith and not his

What about others
After and before you
With no last minute bells to be saved by
Do you ever wonder

Compromise

When we were little
Nobody could tell us that one day
Our life would end
Because we knew different then

Nobody could take our dreams
Down to the basement
To collect dust and be ignored

Nobody punked us out of what was rightfully ours
If we didn't like the way you played
We took our ball and went home

No discussion came because we knew our souls
Were bigger than compromise

For Valerie Bridgeman and Laura Colbert

Yours is the voice that soothes
Wraps its wisdom around my thumping heart
When I have no words to say

Your listen is the quiet
That holds me up
When I could walk into the ocean
And never return to shore

You human me
When I am afraid of my reflection in the river
Who is that woman
With what used to be my face
I remember those hands
Those knees that used to
Bend and reach so free

You blood me
You flesh me
You give me my remember
When I want to run away

You bring me my toes
My legs
Those are my thighs
My breasts and chin
You body me back again

You wing me
You wind me
You song my skin together
I am breath because of you
I am blink and tongue

See these arms and veins
You pray and poem them
Now I am lungs and bones

Because you believed

Rhythm

Tie me into your locs
So I can hear the music in your head
Before the others do
Dance me lightly into your tangle foot groove
We step left foot first then right
Your blood pumps in sync with mine
In ¾ all the time
Because me and you
Is different

Sing me softly with heavy vibrato into your lullabies
I will know right then that you love me
Weave me into your butt naked dreams
Where you are begging me please
To take your hand and follow you into forever

Take me
I wanna go
Make me unafraid to love you back
Loose my inhibitions and I will love you lovely
Giving understanding new
To the stress of our very everyday

When we write
Our world will be transformed

Carmex me beautiful on lips
Full of promises kept
I will speak in cadence often
Of my love never ever ending for you boldly

Vaseline me greasy on knees ashy
From rising always after being knocked unjust

I honor the essence of you
I smell you every time I close my eyes
You lie beautiful beneath me

Walk like a king righteous
I will love
Humble, soon, comfortable
Knowing my back is got

Sit shiva facing me
I massage real life into your scalp

Beeswax sticky on my palms
Tell me you love me
And I will believe

Drift

The gentle squeeze of yours
You try so hard not to break me
But I was broken
Before you came
Are you leaving
Pieces of you behind
For me to smell
And celebrate

Your coming

For Renisha McBride

If I am shot in the face
In the wee hours of the morning
My African and American
Brown freckled body
Dragged onto the table

Will the doctor cut me open
And see that I failed geometry in the tenth grade
Will she lift my guts and know
I sexed a man in the back seat of a car
I never married the father of my son
Will I be a sinner

If she finds merlot
Weed brownies and Trayvon stickers
Spilled down my blouse
Will I be a cunt who deserved to be put out of her
misery
If the doctor runs my credit score
And finds my rating poor
Will it justify my slit throat
My teeth gnashed and bloody jaws

Will the doctor see scars from my abortion
Know that I was bipolar, overweight
And wore a ring in my nose

What will she say about my penchant for cheese and
bread
In the middle of the night
Will she peruse my journals, my blogs
And find bad punctuation
Words against the government

Will she look for Obama posters under my bed
Oscar Grant petitions on top of my bookcase
"This is for Assata" doodled in the margins
Will she turn her smug nose up
To the writers on my wall
Baldwin, Morrison, Walker, Shange

Will she decide that the world has had enuf
Of women like me
With our fists balled up
And hair all kinky

Will she know my dental work and c section
Were paid on the county's dime
How her brows will frown

Will movie tickets from 12 years a slave
Be stuffed down my throat
What will she think of me
In my Malcolm X shirt and fitted blue jeans
Will she imagine sweat and hate and fire
Drip down my nose
As Solomon is beat with a stick
Skin fall from his bones

What will she think of my mother, my father
Who taught me no better
Than to wide hips, thick lips
So black in the night

I know

I know the world will not slow down
No matter how fiercely
I stretch my fists to the sun
I know how to pray
I know I am always praying
No matter my physical position
No matter the words you think you hear
I am always in conversation with Spirit
We converse like two old women
On a Mississippi wooden porch
Chipped paint
Head scarves
Sweet tea
Dogs barking at strangers
Flies at our feet
I know God like that
Don't you

I will take my last breath one day
This is not an if
Before I do I wanna tell these stories

So shut up in my bones
I drag around like wet towels sopping up
Tears my grandmother's mother's mother passed down
Stories that come to me in the night from folks I don't know
Ain't got nothing to do with me
Except they know I know how to get a prayer through
And a story straight

I don't know everything
But I know that getting back to the basics
Is the best business at hand
I know we are nothing without each other
What does it matter all this good I have
If heavy on your mind so muddy
You can't inhale longer than you blink
What good are fancy dresses
And red bottom shoes
If they 'bout to cut off her father's feet

I know sometimes the clouds get low
I know there are days I feel stuck in a mass of
Sadness and fear and anxiety suduku my brain so

math
I forget the numbers to dial
But I know how to reach
I know how to be still
I know how to rock and sing
I know how to cry
I know how to remember how good God's been to me
I know how to wave hand
I know how to give thanks
I know how to close eyes
I know how to know that clouds pass
I know ain't none of this easy
So I know how to give you me
When clouds come to you

I know therapy sessions should be held at Roscoe's
Chicken and Waffles
Over grits and eggs
Prayed over by a greasy hand man with a handkerchief
in his pocket
I know that

I know food ain't free

But I know how to cut mine in four
So we can all eat
I know it's up to me
I know it's up to you
I know I am learning how to forgive
I know that forgiveness does not mean
Stories won't rise
But I know how to let them out
Same one by one way they got in there

I know that I am wonderful
I know that I forget how wonderful I am
I know how to remember the next time I do
I know to open my eyes
And look right into you

Picked

I was never one of those women
Lucky with love
You know the love
The love with fire tongues and rock fingers
Bold enough to hold
That sticky love with bodies that stay

I was always too happy to be chosen
Never the chooser
Always too ready to prove
What a good friend I was
How understanding

See how much I can take
See how fast I forgive
Don't you want a down ass bitch like me
Too quick on the fuck
Too ready with audition sex

See how long I can wait
For your call

For your feelings
Look ma no hands
See how well I ride a dick
Don't you love me yet

You want me to scrub your toilet
Nice and clean
You want your name in a poem
Yo mama need a ride somewhere
Yo sister need a new homegirl
You let me know ok
You
Let
Me
Know

I was only four when I went down on the
neighborhood boy
Girl next door held my head
Made it go up and down
I must have done a real good job
Way he came in my mouth
Way she threatened if I told
I was groomed for you

Preacher man stuck his tongue in my mouth
Sunday after Sunday
Ain't I wife material yet
Count it all joy
Ain't that what the scripture say

You wanna see me not talk back
Eat all my food when you pay
When I said I had a headache
And you said you didn't want to fuck my head anyway
Didn't I grin a little
Like it was funny

Don't you love me yet
Don't you know how tired I am
How retired I am
How out of the game I am
How ready I am to start a forever
With me

Ever

He told his friend
That he could never
Marry a woman like me
At first I was all in my feelings
Then I was like
Wait
He could never

Black like me

I am a woman in the way
Loud
Black
Angry
Free and caged
Diagnosed and unmedicated

I have to watch my tone and dress
It is my fault if I am raped
Way this ass shakes
These titties bounce

Everyone knows I am a whore
Everyone knows I am nothing more
Than a good placeholder
Soon a pretty woman will come along
You can play in her hair
You can see through her skin
You will keep her nice and safe

Everyone knows what a good cook I am

How spotless I keep a house
Keep the children in line too

I stay up late at night
Always available and lucky to get your call
We can talk about racism all night long
Talk about Harriett and Malcolm
Talk about Trayvon and Sandra

Did you see the news today
You see what they did
Everyone knows I know all the news
Everyone knows I keep you laughing
Everyone knows I know my place
With my sensitive self
With my always taking things too personal self
With my extra self
My silly acting self
My attention seeking self

Everyone knows how emotional I am
Everyone knows how much attitude I have
Everyone knows Black women

Don't need as much love
Because we so strong
Because we so built to last
Because we gotta make it

Everyone knows it is best
To put the bills in my name
Everyone knows I keep a few jobs
I keep a few extra dollars
I keep a dime in my purse

Everyone knows my money your money too
Everyone
Everyone
Everyone knows I entertain well
Can keep a smile on my face
A song in my heart
A dance between my toes

Everyone knows bruises don't show up on me
Everyone know how well I take a punch
Everyone
Everyone
Including me

Special thanks to:

my son Uraeus, WomanPreach, Inc.,
The Anansi Writers Workshop, Mama's Kitchen Press

About the Author

Jaha Zainabu is a poet and visual artist from Long Beach, California currently residing in Los Angeles. Jaha has been a member of The Anansi Writers Workshop at The World Stage in Los Angeles, California since 1992. She was the poetry instructor for Say Word and Community Literature Initiative. She was the artist-in-residence for The Girl Blue Project and is currently the artist-in-residence for WomanPreach, Inc. She is also the producer of Red Stories, a storytelling show in Los Angeles. Jaha has traveled throughout the United States performing her poetry. For the past twelve years, she has been the artist-in-residence for WomanPreach, Inc. She has toured her work in many colleges, churches, schools, theaters and poetry venues. Contact Jaha Zainabu at jahazainabu@gmail.com

www.ingramcontent.com/pod-product-compliance
Lightning Source LLC
Chambersburg PA
CBHW030500130626
46549CB00007B/2803